Invertebrates UNDERGROUND

by
Rebecca Phillips-Bartlett

Minneapolis, Minnesota

Credits
All images are courtesy of Shutterstock.com, unless otherwise specified. With thanks to Getty Images, Thinkstock Photo, and iStockphoto. Recurring images – Good_Stock, Guz Anna, Perfect Vectors, Top Vector Studio, Kovalenko Yelyzaveta, GoodStudio, Matiushenko Yelyzaveta. Cover – Paulrommer SL, Eric Isselee, supasart meekumrai, Nick N A, Oleksandr Kostiuchenko. 2–3 – David Jeffrey Ringer. 4–5 – Emvat Mosakovskis, J. Helgason. 6–7 – Klimek Pavol, Leonne Sa Fortes. 8–9 – Ezume Images, Thijs de Graaf, dhilts. 10–11 – galitsin, New Africa. 12–13 – Georgi Baird, Katarina Christenson, Rica Nohara. 14–15 – David James Chatterton, marcophotos. 16–17 – Artush, neohch. 18–19 – Chamois huntress, VladKK, judyjump. 20–21 – GypsyPictureShow, nedomacki. 22–23 – Elvira Tursynbayeva, Twich123.

Bearport Publishing Company Product Development Team
Publisher: Jen Jenson; Director of Product Development: Spencer Brinker; Managing Editor: Allison Juda; Editor: Cole Nelson; Associate Editor: Naomi Reich; Associate Editor: Tiana Tran; Designer: Kim Jones; Designer: Kayla Eggert; Designer: Steve Scheluchin; Production Specialist: Owen Hamlin

Library of Congress Cataloging-in-Publication Data is available at www.loc.gov or upon request from the publisher.

ISBN: 979-8-89577-021-4 (hardcover)
ISBN: 979-8-89577-452-6 (paperback)
ISBN: 979-8-89577-138-9 (ebook)

© 2026 BookLife Publishing
This edition is published by arrangement with BookLife Publishing.

North American adaptations © 2026 Bearport Publishing Company. All rights reserved. No part of this publication may be reproduced in whole or in part, stored in any retrieval system, or transmitted in any form or by any means, electronic, mechanical, photocopying, recording, or otherwise, without written permission from the publisher. Bearport Publishing is a division of FlutterBee Education Group.

For more information, write to Bearport Publishing, 5357 Penn Avenue South, Minneapolis, MN 55419.

CONTENTS

Minibeasts Underground 4
Ants 6
Pill Bugs 8
Earthworms 10
Cicadas 12
Bees 14
Cockroaches 16
Grubs 18
Beetles 20
So Many Minibeasts 22
Glossary 24
Index 24

MINIBEASTS
UNDERGROUND

Hello there! I am Molly Mole. I dig for food underground near my **burrow**. I eat mostly small **invertebrates**, such as **insects** and worms.

An invertebrate is an animal with no backbone.

I like calling these small animals minibeasts. They are my favorite foods. Let's dig down and see what we can find underground!

Are you ready to meet some minibeasts?

ANTS

Ants live in underground nests. These nests have many tunnels and rooms.

Ants leave behind a trail of smells for other ants to follow.

Ants live in large groups called colonies. Each colony has a queen ant. Most of the other ants work together to care for the queen.

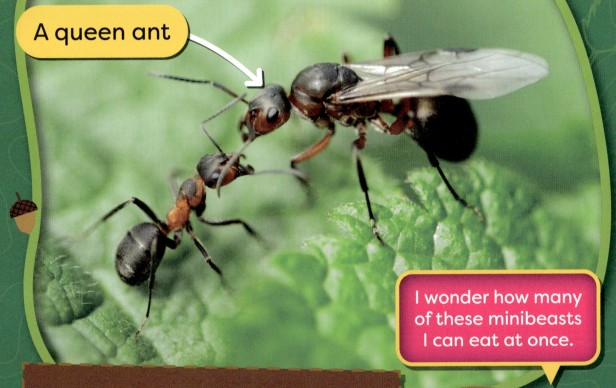

A queen ant

I wonder how many of these minibeasts I can eat at once.

FACT FILE

Size: Up to 1 inch (2.5 cm) long
Diet: Plants, fungi, and other insects
Habitat: Dry and open areas

PILL BUGS

Pill bugs are known by many different names. Some people call them roly-polies because they can roll themselves into a ball. Others call them wood lice.

Mother pill bugs have a pouch for their babies, just like kangaroos!

A pill bug is a type of animal called a **crustacean** (kruh-STAY-schuhn). Most crustaceans live in water. However, pill bugs live mostly underground.

FACT FILE

Size: Up to 0.8 in. (2 cm) long
Diet: Plants, fungi, and algae
Habitat: Everywhere except polar regions

EARTHWORMS

Earthworms eat dead plants in dirt.

Earthworms do an important job as they wiggle in the dirt. They move **nutrients** around underground. This helps keep the soil healthy so plants can grow.

An earthworm's body is made up of many ring-shaped sections. Each section is covered in tiny hairs that help it move and dig.

Earthworms are slimy!

FACT FILE

Size: Up to 14 in. (36 cm) long

Diet: Rotting leaves and plants

Habitat: Moist soils with lots of rotting plants

CICADAS

Adult cicadas are noisy insects. However, before they become loud adults, they spend most of their lives underground. These young cicadas, called **nymphs**, can live underground for up to 17 years.

A cicada nymph

Eventually, cicada nymphs crawl out of the ground and climb nearby trees or buildings. Then, they shed their skins and become adult cicadas.

FACT FILE

Size: Up to 1.5 in. (4 cm) long
Diet: Sap
Habitat: Forests, grasslands, and deserts

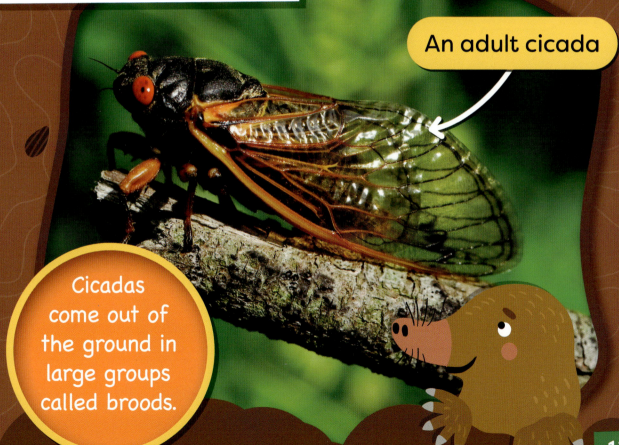

An adult cicada

Cicadas come out of the ground in large groups called broods.

BEES

Pollen

Bees are very important! They eat nectar made by plants. As they move between plants, they spread pollen. This helps more plants grow.

Say nectar like NEK-tur.

Some bees live above the ground in homes called hives. However, most of the world's bees live in underground burrows.

A mining bee

FACT FILE

Size: Up to 3 in. (7 cm) long

Diet: Nectar, pollen, and honey

Habitat: Forests, fields, wetlands, and deserts

COCKROACHES

Cockroaches live all around the world. Some even live in the Arctic! These minibeasts dig around to find rotting plants and wood.

Cockroaches have been around for more than 320 million years!

Cockroaches lose a little water every time they breathe. To save water, they will hold their breath for more than 40 minutes at a time.

FACT FILE

Size: Up to 2 in. (5 cm) long
Diet: Rotting plants
Habitat: Tropical and mild climates worldwide

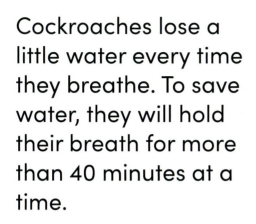

These minibeasts are chewy!

17

GRUBS

Beetles start their lives as grubs. Grubs can live underground for many years, eating plant roots and leaves to help them grow.

Many grubs are small and white.

Grubs help keep soil healthy. They leave behind healthy nutrients after they eat. Many animals dig up grubs for food.

FACT FILE

Size: Up to 9 in. (23 cm) long
Diet: Plant roots and leaves
Habitat: Everywhere except Antarctica and high mountains

BEETLES

Once a grub has grown big enough, it becomes an adult beetle. There are more than 300,000 known types of beetles. Many of them continue to live underground as adults.

A ground beetle

All beetles have a pair of hard top wings and a pair of softer lower wings for flying.

Beetles use their **antennae** to learn about their surroundings. These long body parts can touch, smell, and taste things around them.

Antennae

Beetles don't see very well. Neither do moles, like me!

FACT FILE

Size: Up to 7.5 in. (19 cm) long

Diet: Plants, other insects, snails, tadpoles, and dung

Habitat: Everywhere except Antarctica and high mountains

SO MANY MINIBEASTS

The soil is full of food to help minibeasts grow. An underground home is also a safe place to hide from many **predators**.

Lots of minibeasts help keep the soil healthy for plants and animals.

These adorable minibeasts make a perfect mole meal. Take a look in the dirt next time you are outside. You might find a minibeast hiding nearby!

Which underground minibeast was your favorite?

GLOSSARY

antennae body parts on an insect's head used for feeling, tasting, and smelling

burrow a hole or tunnel dug by an animal to live in

crustacean an animal that is part of a group with hard exoskeletons and jointed legs

insects small animals that have six legs, an exoskeleton, two antennae, and three main body parts

invertebrates animals without backbones

nutrients vitamins, minerals, and other substances needed by living things for health and growth

nymphs the young of some types of insects, such as cicadas

predators animals that hunt and eat other animals

INDEX

antennae 21
burrows 4, 15
leaves 11, 18–19
nymphs 12–13
plants 7, 9–11, 14, 16–19, 21–22
pollen 14–15
predators 22
soil 10, 19, 22
trees 13
wings 20